T0197647

AuthorHouse™
1663 Liberty Drive
Bloomington, IN 47403
www.authorhouse.com
Phone: 833-262-8899

Because of the dynamic nature of the Internet, any web addresses or links contained
in this book may have changed since publication and may no longer be valid. The views
expressed in this work are solely those of the author and do not necessarily reflect the
views of the publisher, and the publisher hereby disclaims any responsibility for them.

Any people depicted in stock imagery provided by Getty Images are models,
and such images are being used for illustrative purposes only.
Certain stock imagery © Getty Images.

This book is printed on acid-free paper.

ISBN: 978-1-6655-3136-8 (sc)
ISBN: 978-1-6655-3137-5 (hc)
ISBN: 978-1-6655-3135-1 (e)

Print information available on the last page.

Published by AuthorHouse 07/13/2021

authorHOUSE®

This book was inspired by and created for my son, Jude. The pages brought to be by joining our imaginations together one night during bedtime. My message to him and to you all, is to always listen to the small things in life and to be in every moment. You never know what might come from it.

One day in a far away place, lived people of all sorts. There were giants that were as tall as the clouds and little bean people that were so small you needed a magnifying glass just to see them.

Once a week, all the giants got together and threw huge parties where they ate, danced and laughed for hours.

Their favorite food is beans....

Now as you can imagine, giants as tall as the clouds with stomachs as big as a small car, needed a lot of beans.

With the bean fields growing scarce from all the eating each week, the giants had to adventure out to new lands in order to find new fields.

After searching for 3 days, they found the most beautiful field any of the giants had ever seen. They quickly picked several baskets and went home.

Once getting home, the giants gave all the beans to the wisest and most skillful cook of them all, grandmother giant Mary. She knew all there was to know about cooking.

She grabbed the biggest cooking pot she had and put the beans in. She then added some spices and vegetables from her garden and put it over the fire.

Just then all the beans burst open and out popped the tiniest people grandmother giant had ever seen.

They looked up and yelled, "STOP...please do not eat us, we are people too and these beans are our houses"

Grandmother giant was so shocked she yelled out in excitement, "Ahhhhh" but quickly helped the bean people up and onto the counter and apologized. "I'm so sorry, we didn't know you lived in these beans"

The bean people replied, "That's ok, we love beans too" They then offered to help the giants find new beans they all could eat.

The giants searched high…. The bean people searched low…..

And at last, they found beans they could eat.

Grandmother giant checked the beans for any people and started cooking them with all her vegetables and spices until they were the best beans ever.

They all sat down and ate. The giants danced like never before and the bean people danced inside their homes, making the beans jump all across the floor. They laughed.

It was a night like never before.....

Printed in the United States
by Baker & Taylor Publisher Services